Maya's First Rose

Maya's First Rose

Diary of a Very Special Love

by
Martin Scot Kosins

Illustrations By Howard Fridson
With a Foreword by Burl Ives

OPEN SKY BOOKS   ROYAL OAK・MICHIGAN

Published by Open Sky Books
600 West Eleven Mile Road, Suite A
Royal Oak, Michigan 48067

Text Copyright© 1992 by Martin Scot Kosins
Illustrations Copyright© 1992 by Howard Fridson
All Rights Reserved.
No part of this book may be reproduced or
transmitted in any form or by any means,
electronic or mechanical, including photocopying,
recording, or by any information storage and retrieval system,
without permission in writing from the publisher.

Printed in
94   93   92   92   91   4321

ISBN 0-9634380-0-X

Designed and illustrated by Howard Fridson

Maya's First Rose is printed on High Quality Acid-Free Recycled Paper.

TO MAYA
WHO HAD THE GENTLEST HEART
AND
DR. MICHAEL PINTAR
WHO HELPED KEEP IT BEATING

My heartfelt thanks to

> MEHER BABA

for inspiring me to write
Maya's First Rose,

> SUSIE FILIP

who worked hard to type and help me
polish the manuscript,

> CLEVELAND AMORY

whose generous praise encouraged me
to seek a publisher,

> and especially

> JOYCE JEROW

who entered my life at its lowest point—
who encouraged and cheered me—
and whose belief in me helped me find
my way back to creativity.

Martin Scot Kosins

CONTENTS

A FOREWORD BY BURL IVES 11

DIARY OF A VERY SPECIAL LOVE 15

AN AFTERWORD 99

A FOREWORD

A heart warming tale of truth told with delicacy and finesse. *Maya*, a big huggable dog, came into Marty's life and thereby the group spirit of the animal kingdom was raised.

Animals, dogs especially, bring us so much unconditional love. I have four dogs at present, have had as many as six a few years back. Mamasita, 16 years, still enjoying good health, came to my wife, Dorothy, and me in Mexico nine years ago. This mixed-breed, sorry looking dog came to our condo door, wounded and sick. We nursed her back to health. She then proceeded to thank us by going upstairs to the Roman tub and having nine puppies. Her daughter, Evita, is with us today, though we lost her son, Chilli Pepper, a few months back. Both Mamasita and Evita are beauties with lovely silk coats and big beautiful brown eyes.

Heidi is our magnificent 12 year old Shepherd who follows Dorothy around like a huge hovering

angel. The newest addition is a mischievious two year old apricot poodle, Ashley Adorable, who in turn, follows Heidi. . . So Dorothy has two protectors while the two Mexicans hang out with me.

So you see, I can relate to Marty's journey with *Maya*, with the fun filled frolicking years of her youth and also with the sad years of her decline.

How empty this world would be without our animal friends to teach us the meaning of devotion. Bravo Martin Scot Kosins. The animal lovers of the world salute you and place a rose at your feet!

Burl Ives

Diary of a
Very Special Love

Maya

I truly don't remember when Maya stopped being a Dog, and became very much more to me.

Perhaps it was around the time of her first operation, nearly ten years ago.

What I do know for sure is that, in the time we were together, Maya became the most important thing on this earth to me.

At one time, in my life, my career seemed most important. But as Maya grew old, and became frail, I realized that I would even give up my career for her—and I did. I realize now that even my life would have been little to sacrifice, for the huge amounts of love that Maya gave me each moment of her life.

Now, it is almost midnight of New Year's Eve, and a New Year will soon arrive. It will be the first time in seventeen years that I will greet a New Year without Maya at my side. For Maya was *always* at my side.

As I gaze out the window, I can see the pale Winter moon shining down through the leafless branches of the trees, casting its light on the smooth layer of newly fallen snow. And the Winter wind is howling against the windowpanes.

But in my mind. . .

In my mind the warm Autumn sun is shining through branches which are heavy with the almost fallen leaves. There is gold in the air. And Maya, in her red and black plaid woolen coat, and in her prime, is walking faster than any Dog has ever walked—pulling me behind her. The crackle of yellow leaves hits the air with each motion of her beautiful tan and white paws. And the Autumn breeze fluffs and brushes the hair on her neck. And as I glance at the ground—as we hurry along—I see our shadow. It is a shadow of me, larger than life or time, with Maya at my side.

Maya was *always* at my side.

I didn't really want a Dog.

It seemed to me that a new wife, and a career as a musician, were quite enough responsibility for a young man.

But, my new wife insisted—she insisted on a lot of things. So, one day I gave in, and found myself in a little pet shop looking into a cage of not so little dogs.

There were four of them, all from the same litter. They all looked pretty much the same, but for one difference. One of them was drinking from a bowl of water, with her back foot standing in a second bowl of water.

I never saw her face, but I said to the owner, "That's the one." Before my new wife could ever agree or disagree, the Dog was paid for and in my arms.

I named her Maya, the East Indian word for a dream or something that seems unreal. That day seems unreal to me now because it was so long ago. I was twenty-four then. I am over forty now.

Looking back, I realize that we can never guess what will be important in our lives. And we certainly can never know how much we will love someone.

I also realize how much the hand of fate—even the hand of God—was working for me and Maya that special day.

Five years later, the relationship with my new wife was over. But my relationship with Maya was just beginning—

No one could ever guess exactly what breed Maya was. But everyone agreed that she was very beautiful.

There was never a time, when we were sitting in the park, or walking near our home, that people didn't come up to admire the Big Dog with the gentle face.

Children especially wanted to meet her. And if she sensed that a child might be a little afraid of dogs, she would lower her head just a little until the child decided to approach her. She would stay very still until the first tentative touch. Then, she would look up at the child with her warmest and happiest smile—yes, Maya actually did smile, you know.

When she was most content, she would open her mouth wide with her lips drawn way back and curling toward the sky.

If you touched her ears, she would tilt her head upwards. And even though she would close her eyes, all but for a little bit, they would be gleaming—as if they were filled with stars.

No child in the world could be afraid of her then.

While they patted and hugged her, I would explain to children that Maya was actually a combina-

tion of Boxer and Shepherd. The Boxer was in her body, with her broad shoulders and large strong chest. The Shepherd could be seen in her face, with its slender nose and noble jaw. There were times when she looked as elegant as a Princess—and other times when she seemed as playful as a new born baby. And even though she grew to be very old, she never lost the sparkle or humor that people love in a puppy.

Maya's license described her as a tricolor. It is true that she was "tan-white-black." But that only tells part of the story.

She really was the color of pure, deep, honey, and the black and white hair that peppered her coat gave her a rich vibrant shine.

Each paw was tipped with white, as if she were wearing satin dress shoes.

At her chin began a patch of white that continued down her neck. As it reached her chest it broadened to cover her entire front, like a tuxedo shirt on a well dressed entertainer.

The black was all on her muzzle, tipped by a nose of silk. But as she grew old the black surrounding her face turned to white. Beginning first at the front, then more and more and further back, until her entire face was white as snow, even around her eyes. The only black left was just beneath her nose. And if you looked at her in a certain way, it seemed that she had a Charlie Chaplin moustache.

At times I called her "my beautiful white face." For her face was indeed beautiful, and her eyes so soulful. As the years flew by they filled with untold amounts of love for me.

More than once she had operations on those eyes, which left them cratered and scarred. Time also turned their coffee brown to a creamy glaze. And of course they lost most of their sight. But they could always see me—and the stars remained bright and shone like jewels through the mist of age.

And through those eyes I felt as if I could see the pureness of Love in its most precious form. Unconditional and given with no thought of return.

I know that the thing we humans call The Soul really does exist. I saw it—in the eyes of an Old Dog.

Maya had no tail.

Whoever trimmed the tails of the litter she was from, certainly did a quick and careless job.

So, when she walked, from behind she looked more like a small deer than a dog.

But what she lacked in tail, she made up for in

ears. For even when they stood up, the tips would bend over—like a hat of a General in the Italian Army.

How important those ears were to us in her final year.

From the very first, she had the habit of quickly turning her head from side to side, just when she woke up from a nap, or wanted to change her position. When she turned her head, her ears would sharply cut the air, and the sound they made was like flags flapping in the wind.

Wherever I was in the house, I could hear her ears flap and know she was up and moving about.

What was a cute gesture became a vital message.

For in her last days, when she no longer walked alone, and needed help to find a comfortable position, I would hear her ears flapping, and would run to her side.

Nature gave Maya other gifts as well.

She had a voice like musical thunder. More than once her bark kept unwanted intruders from our house.

Each night at midnight, she would stand before me like a watchdog, and begin a low growl which came from deep in her chest.

I would ask her what she wanted, and the mock growl became a series of sounds which could be heard several houses away.

Then, the question she had waited to hear all evening: "Do you want to raid the cookie jar?"

Small leaps of her front feet off the ground, now accompanied the game.

Together, imitating burglars, we would sneak

down the hall to the huge cookie jar in the kitchen, which was always bursting with treats.

Together, back in the front room, we would settle down to watch Charlie Chan on the late movie, until the hours of dawn which are a musician's bedtime.

Not until a poke in the face with her mighty nose, would I awake the next day.

Nature's greatest blessing to Maya was probably the strong Spirit of her body, which helped her to fight the battles which came with age.

It seems that she was old for so long, that her youth nearly left my memory forever.

What a shock to find an old photo of Maya young and strong—standing proudly on all four legs.

For with all the gifts, nature stopped short on Maya's hind legs.

They were delicate and fragile. Much more suited to a dog half her size and weight, her slender legs became ever more important to us through the years.

First they created a bond between Maya and me, which I had never known with any living creature on this earth.

Later, they sealed that bond—and drew me closer to Maya than I can ever hope to be again, with anyone.

When the sun was warm in the sky of her youth, Maya would sit beneath it for hours—raising her head to catch the passing breezes.

Our yard was her world.

There were always birds for her to chase. And she was always careful never to catch any—so that they would return to play the game again.

She could easily make the ground shake by running upon it.

She could easily imitate lightning by escaping the yard each night to attack every neighboring garbage bag.

She could easily let me know when her snack of buttered toast was ready, by waiting for the flip of the toaster oven door.

She could easily have let the house burn down, the night she watched the flames whip from the overheated toaster oven, when the door did not flip open.

She ate the hose.

She ate a rubber toy.

She ate the rubber mat beneath the oriental carpet, and carefully replaced the carpet when she was through.

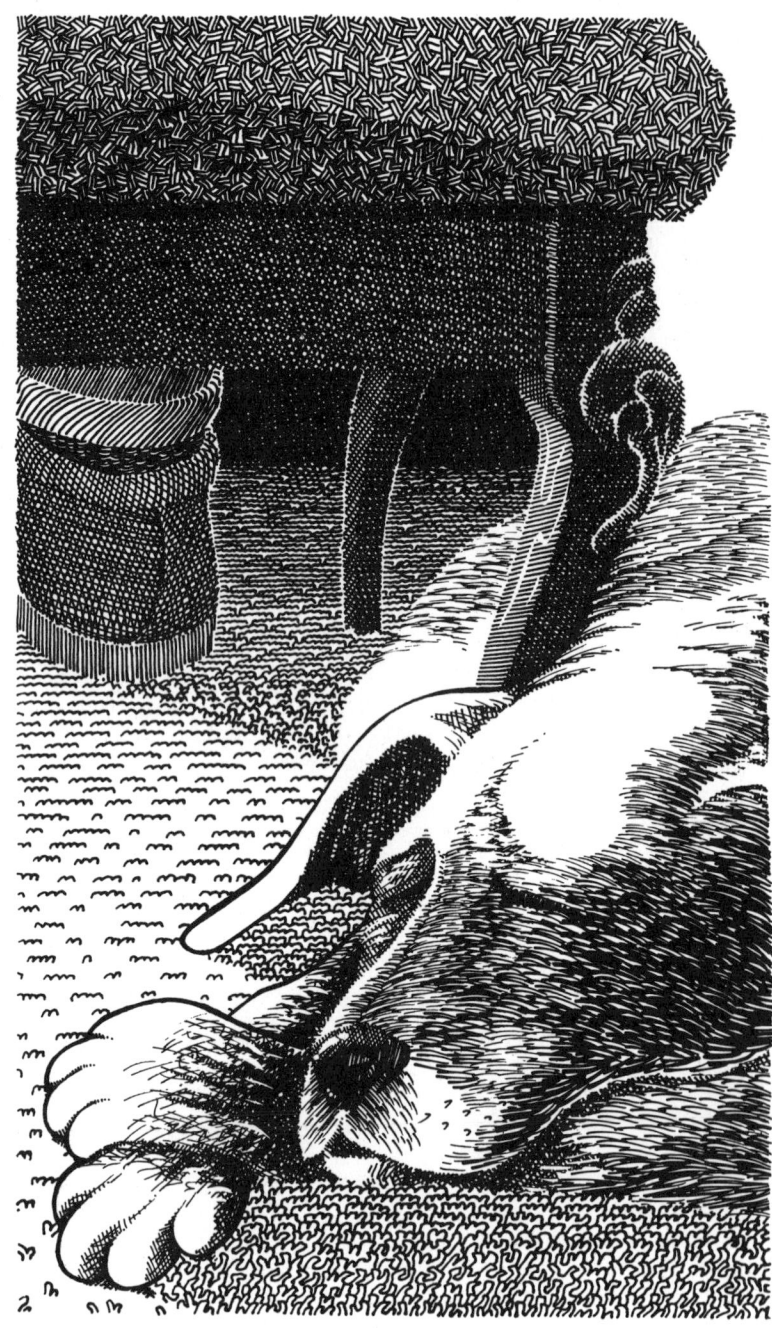

She had rubber balls, and a pipe, and hard rubber rings which she loved to toss and catch.

She could eat and play endlessly. Her energy never seemed to stop—except for the music.

Somehow, miraculously, Maya knew from our first moments together, what music meant to me.

Her first night home was filled with exploration. She ran through the rooms and halls of her barely furnished new house. I could do nothing to stop her from jumping around—so I decided to practice.

Sitting at the small piano, I began to play. I looked down.

Maya was there.

Under the piano, her head nearly touching the pedal, she had found her spot and was listening.

Very soon she was too large for that place, and had moved to a place under the bench.

A few months later, grown to her full size, she could be found at the side of the bench—cozily snuggled near its legs and the soft bottom of the couch nearby.

No matter the time of day or night,
No matter what she was doing,
When I went to the piano,
Maya went with me.

Hour after hour, for sixteen years, though other things in our lives changed, our places by the piano remained the same.

I haven't taken my place at the piano for a long long time.

But a beam from the warm sun of her youth, still glows in Maya's spot, at the side of the bench.

In the endless days since Maya left, I have often thought, "What price would I pay to see her smile again, for even five minutes time."

The answer is that no price would be too high.

There is no price that can be placed on Time. And there is no value which can be given, on a heart filled with Love.

The last year of Maya's life—with little other company, and no release from our seclusion—seemed to last much less than a minute.

Each single day since her leaving—with total freedom to come and go and live my life—seems to last much more than a year.

The price for love may well be loneliness. And perhaps the value of having a full heart, can only be found when we lose a part of it, forever.

If I had ever loved a person, the way I loved Maya, I would have considered it a miracle. The love I felt for Maya, was surely more—it was God's gift to the beauty of my life.

As long as I live I will remember a moment in which time stood still.

An old record, by my favorite musician, was playing. I was standing by the record player watching the record turn. The smoke from my favorite pipe filled the room, and blended with the twilight.

I looked down, and there was Maya. Lying peacefully on the bright orange rug, her head still and her breathing steady.

A quiet thought entered my mind,

"Maya, we're still together."

Just then, she looked at me—

and time stopped.

What I felt could only be described as Peace. The kind of Peace I had read about in Ancient Books. A Peace which entered my heart and never left.

And I remember thinking, "If a hand came down from Heaven, and lifted me off the earth—I could go quietly, peacefully and with no sorrow at all."

I can feel that same Peace again, each time I think of Maya, and the joy we found in each other.

The Miracle has become a fact—a gift of radiant Peace has become my own. What some search for throughout an entire lifetime, I have received in the middle of my life.

When Maya left, she took a large part of my heart along.

It was the part filled with childhood and joy and music.

What I have left is the corner of my heart which is filled with Maya.

The part which is filled with the sound of the Autumn leaves as we walked, and the glow of setting suns upon us.

Having to lose so much of my heart, must be the price I have to pay for Peace.

I certainly don't mind at all.
A small corner of a heart,
filled with Maya,
seems to be
all the heart I need.

Spring was here.

As you can imagine, my walks with Maya had now become very special to me.

Much more than just "taking the Dog out."

Watching the expression on her face as she walked, became one of my great joys in life.

Of course, Maya still thought she was a puppy— so I had to pace her. I would hold the leash tightly, to keep her from walking too fast. When I "threw her ball," it was really just a roll of a few inches.

When she grabbed her ring, to toss it around and leap for it, I would try to stop her in time.

People told me I was "babying" her. But I knew differently.

To my goals of success and happiness I had added one more: the goal of keeping Maya with me for as long as I could.

With that new goal came a promise: each day of Maya's life would be the happiest day that any creature on earth could have.

Yet, sometimes the puppy in her won out. She would tear across the yard, after a squirrel, before I could stop her.

This was the only thing that would make me lose my temper. Before I knew it, I was shouting, "You run across the yard and I get the heartache! Do you know what will happen if you ruin your legs? *I'm* the one who will suffer!"

Then I would see that her legs had become stiff from running.

Right away I would be on the floor next to her—apologizing and asking her to please forgive me.

Her giant tongue would lick my face, and I knew that she had ignored me all along.

All that I gained was a frozen fear that came over me, and would not go away until the stiffness in her legs went away.

In a day or two the stiffness would leave, and we would be walking together again. We would walk the long path beside the golf course, in back of our home.

We would walk down the street, where everyone we saw would stop to tell me how beautiful she looked.

Later, we would walk up our block, to the little park on the corner. There we would sit beneath a tree. Together, we would watch Spring become Summer, and Summer become Fall.

Those were beautiful, happy days.

Maya sat in her favorite place by the front room window, and watched me put the big bike away for the last time.

It was a shiny red "three-wheeler," with a black seat, and a large basket in the back.

A few years before, sitting with Maya in the same spot, we watched a neighbor and his dog race by. The neighbor was on a bicycle, the dog, filled with glee, running by his side.

I had never learned to ride a two-wheel bike, but I wanted Maya to have the fun of running beside one. So, I looked for, and found, the big three-wheeler.

What a sight we were. Me, looking like a big kid on an oversized tricycle, Maya, at the end of her leash, running so fast and hard that I could barely keep up. Soon I could stop pedaling, and the strength in Maya's body would pull me and the bike along at such a terrific speed, that the wind would pin my hair and her ears back against our heads.

The window in the front room was large and low. It was Maya's window on the world. Even more, it was her constant station where she watched me leave the house, and waited for my return.

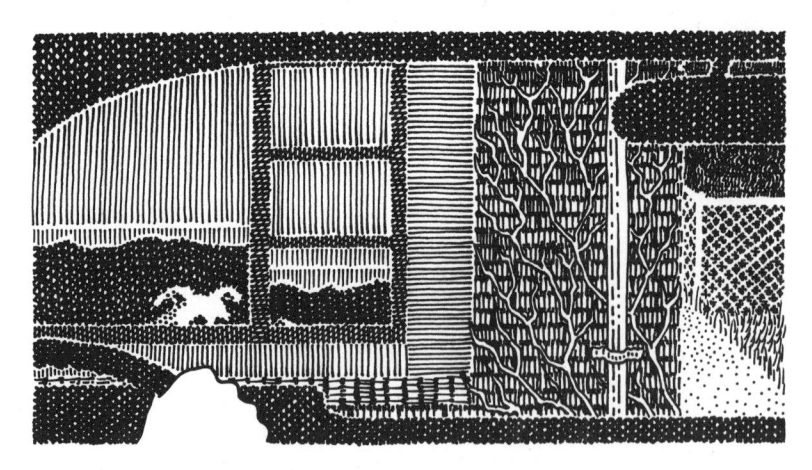

When I would leave, she would be at the front door. By the time I was down the walk, I would see her at the window, her eyes following me as I crossed the lawn.

As I would start the car, I could see her body disappear. And as I drove away, I could see her ears and her eyes—just above the windowsill.

Turning my head back toward the house, I saw the top of her head turn to follow me.

The mystery to me is how Maya, like a mystic, always seemed to know when I was coming back.

Whether I was gone for one hour—for five hours—or for the whole day—she was already sitting up, her eyes sharply focused on the soon to appear car.

Before the engine had stopped, she was dancing in circles by the front door—giving me the welcome that made me feel like a King.

And on the chillywarm Autumn days, back at the window in a split second, Maya would watch me cross the lawn once more. This time she would be standing, because she knew that I would soon reappear with the big red bike. Within the next minute we would be running and riding against the Autumn wind.

Of course, I knew that Maya's running days were behind her. Now, she would usually nap in the hours of the Autumn twilight.

Quietly, not waking her,
I went to the garage for the bike.
Past the car, down the driveway, and I was on.
With the first turn of the pedals,
I glanced toward the house.
Maya was at the window—sitting—
her eyes very still.
With the motion of a very small circle,
I was back in the driveway and off the bike.

Soon the shiny red three-wheeler would be covered with dust and cobwebs in a corner of the garage.

Maya had not moved. When I came back into the house, I sat beside her and looked out of the window.

In the silence I could hear the sounds of the first Autumn winds.

And as I saw the first yellow leaves drifting from the birch in the front yard, I wondered just how ten years could have passed so quickly.

And I thought of all the changes that those ten years had brought to Maya and me.

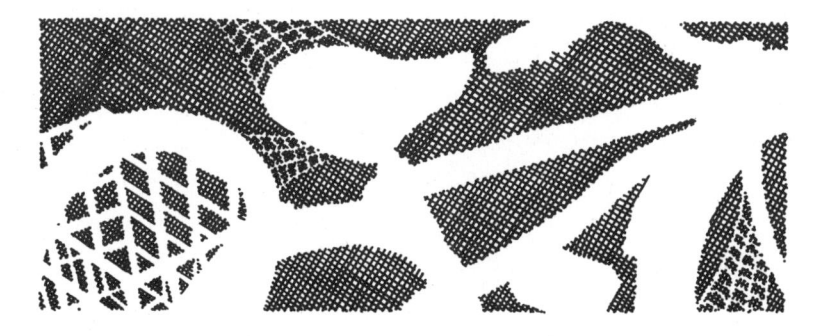

It was Winter.

Maya was turning ten.

She had gotten used to her back legs being a little stiff, from time to time. It didn't seem to bother her, and she didn't complain.

But one day I noticed that she was not bending her legs at all. She was hobbling, and her legs were like brittle wood.

The usual aspirins and cortisone didn't help, and Dr. Mike, her Veterinarian, decided that Maya should see a specialist.

The drive to the clinic at Michigan State University was not a long one, but it seemed to take hours.

Maya was not afraid. She watched the snow covered trees go by, not moving once the whole time.

I didn't notice the trees. But I did notice that something inside me began to close.

When I heard the word "operation," it felt as if a metal door had slammed upon my heart.

Driving home, I saw the trees.

They were bleak and bare.

I realized for the first time, that this was not a Dog, a pet, I was leaving behind.

It was a part of me.

As dear as my heart was to my body, that is how dear Maya had become to my life.

Days as long as months went by.

When I saw Maya next, she was wearing two huge casts on her hind legs.

For the first time ever, I lifted her in my arms.

For the first of a thousand times,
I lifted her into the car.

For the first of what must have been
millions of times,
I carried her
from place to place in our home—
carried her outside—
carried her in.

Always so very careful.

After all, it was my heart I was carrying.

When the casts came off, Maya began to walk again.

She was almost as good as new.

The wind still blew on our faces. Only now, we felt it coming through the windows of the car.

Around and around the neighborhood, we would take our evening drive. In the back seat, Maya would close her eyes and lift her head, to taste the breeze.

After a while I would pull onto the main road, and Maya would sit up with the anticipation and excitement of a child.

The Dairy Queen was just moments away.

Parents and children alike, would pause by the car to watch the Big Dog in the back seat—devouring a huge ice cream cone.

The stars would shine.

We would go home to our place by the piano.

I wouldn't have to leave now, like I used to.

For many years I would leave the house each evening at six.

By seven o'clock I would be playing the piano in one of the fancy restaurants around the city.

Of course, I liked being a musician.

But I *loved* being a composer.

I was very serious about success and fame.

School for a masters degree in the daytime,

Performing for a living at night,
Composing, for my true ambitions,
in the early hours of the morning.
And people liked my music.
My stars grew closer.
Now, instead of leaving the house to play piano each night, I wrote music for small groups and large symphony orchestras.
I arranged music for records and radio commercials.
I received commissions and royalties.
And I read my name in the papers.
Although I was busier than ever,
I built my own schedule.
Maya and I added new outings to our rides and walks.
Trips to the cider mill, for donuts.
Visits to friends' homes for dinners.
Good company, and even a special girlfriend,
for parties at our own home.
Work and life were one.
And always there were those moments which I treasure now, more than any achievement of those very special years.

The moments between the work and fun, when beneath the crystal blue star filled skies of early morning, I would find myself looking at Maya.

I realize now that my truest inner voice was speaking to my heart, in those still and quiet moments.

It was preparing me for the most important test of my life. It was whispering, "The feeling of love for any living thing, means more to the heart than any fame can bring."

Mr. Foley, the handyman, hammered and sawed beneath the warm early Autumn sun.

The children watched from the street on their way home from school.

Maya watched from her window.

With the beauty and wisdom of age, she had accepted the stiffness in her back legs.

Our walks had grown shorter.

And she found her own way of going up the steps of our front porch.

She took each step by placing her front paws first, then lifting her hind legs—together—after her.

It worked for a while, but as time passed this grew harder for her.

I began to notice she was out of breath at the end of our walks.

So the walks became shorter—and I called Mr. Foley.

After two days he was done.

The neighbors wondered if I had broken a leg. Some asked if I had taken in an elderly or handicapped person—perhaps my grandmother.

On the third day—as they returned from school—

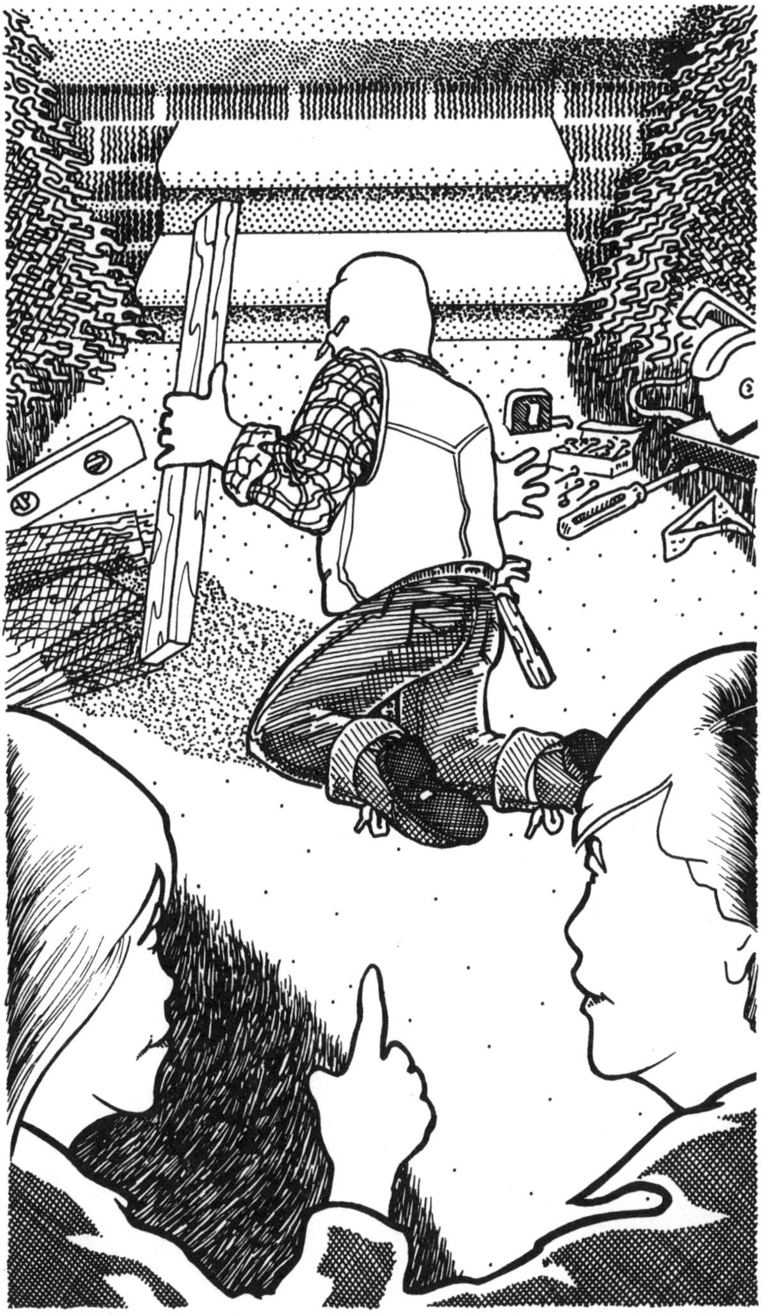

the children were the first to see what the ramps were for.

They smiled with delight as the Big Dog who lived in the yellow house, learned to walk up and down the new ramp where the steps had been.

"No danger of falling," I told Maya. The carpet would prevent that.

Just a glide, and we were on our walk again.

In the backyard, the ramp was longer and had extensions to both sides.

Just a turn to the right or the left, and she would be on any side of the yard she pleased.

No more steps to climb for Maya.

Together, we would do all we could to make a friend of Time, and fight the coming of Age.

"Two chicken dinners, with all the trimmings, to go please."

It was the happiest day of my life, and we were celebrating.

Unbelievably, Maya was fifteen.

It had been a while since she had eaten regular dog food.

When Dr. Mike discovered that she had developed an enlarged heart, he put her on a special "senior citizens" diet.

Everyday I would boil the hamburger, and mix it with the low-salt kibble prescription dog food.

Her treat became toast of no-salt bread.

I refused to believe that she was old.

Even with her legs becoming more and more fragile, and her hair becoming grey, she was a *young* fifteen.

The rhythm of my own life had become faster and faster.

More projects,

More trips.

And more people, well known and famous, became my friends and acquaintances.

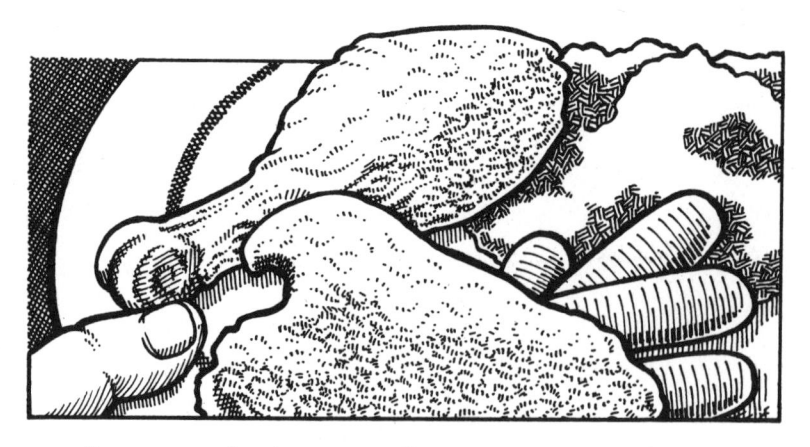

I was producing two albums at once. I flew from the West Coast to the East Coast and back again.

This time, my best friend Tom stayed with Maya.

I knew she was well taken care of, but my mind was restless. A part of me always wanted to finish the work and return home quickly.

Meeting the Beautiful Actress in New York didn't help things at all.

It had been a long time since I had met anyone as charming and as nice.

And it had been a long time since I cared for anyone.

She had just broken up with her boyfriend and I could see that she liked me very much.

When I returned home, exhausted from the pace of my work, Maya greeted me at the door with a look in her eyes which I had never seen before.

She would not leave my side.

It had grown hard for her to get up and lay down. But she moved with me from room to room. Even if I was gone for a few moments I would look around and see her following me.

I began to tell her to "stay" if I had to leave the room. But more often I would try to not leave her in a room alone.

I would think of everything I needed at that time, and bring it with us on the first trip.

Every week I spoke to the Beautiful Actress.
Christmas was coming—
She had been invited to parties
by all her famous friends.
Before she made any plans, she was wondering—
Would I be in New York for the holidays?
How I wanted to go—how I wanted to see her.
How, I wondered, could I leave—
Some deep voice inside of me told me I could not.
I was soon to find out why.
Sometimes we can not have two kinds of happiness.
We have to choose the thing which will mean the most to us in our life.

The deep voice told me my happiness was here.
And indeed,
I was happy,
Although sorry to have lost what might have been between the Actress and me.

As I watched Maya devour the chicken and mashed potatoes and carrots of her birthday dinner, I realized that some choices are really made for us.

I thought I had made a decision to stay home with Maya.
The deep voice of my heart
was telling me
my decision was made for me,
fifteen
long
years
ago.

"Peg—"

My voice broke into a million pieces.

My dear friend Peg was listening carefully on the other end of the phone. But she couldn't quite hear what I was trying to say, through a flood of tears.

I said it again.

"Peg—I think I will have to put Maya to sleep."

I had just come from Peg's house. We had dinner together.

Just before I left, Maya had tripped a little coming up the ramp. I thought she had just missed a step, so I fed her and left.

Now, she couldn't stand or walk.

There was a dazed look in her eyes.

Peg could say nothing to console me.

Maya devoured the cookies I fed her.

Yet, she could hardly move.

I lay down on the floor and held her until she slept.

I got a blanket and pillow for myself, and lay beside her until dawn.

I prayed.

I made coffee.

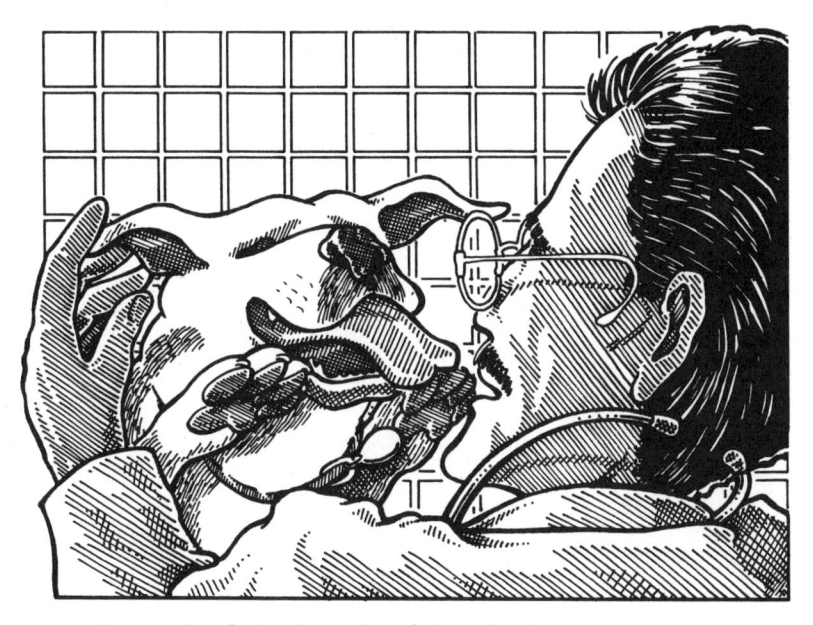

I watched the hands of the clock creep to the nine and the twelve.

I lifted Maya into the car.

I listened to Dr. Mike say, "A stroke."

I learned that dogs can have strokes, just as people can. And that they can recover.

After the shot, I brought Maya home.

My door closed.

My phone closed.

My heart opened, and I prayed.

If there were any pain for her to experience, Dear God, let me bear it for her.

And I vowed.

If she gets well, I will never leave town again—no matter what offer or reason.

And I pledged to Heaven,

I will never leave Maya home alone, for more time than absolutely necessary.

Whatever part of my life I held in reserve for myself, now became Maya's.

I realized that her love for me had taught me about Love itself.

I became aware that the comfort of having her near, had sustained me through all sorts of events.

The grocery delivered the food.

The drugstore delivered the odds and ends.

I stayed home.

In the frozen dead of a Michigan Winter, at any hour of the day or night, I lifted her seventy pounds in my arms when she needed to go out.

I carried her down the ramp,
Supported her after gently placing her on the ground,
Lifted her,
And carried her back up the ramp once more.
I was changing inside.
Something about me was different.
I always thought I was truly devoted to my music.
Maya was teaching me what true Devotion really means.
Days and nights went by.
And Maya—once again,
like a little clumsy puppy—
began to walk—
a step at a time. . .

I had heard the word "blessing" all my life. The next two years taught me what it meant.

Since she had turned fifteen, I looked upon each day Maya was with me as a true gift. Each day was teaching me that a moment, especially a moment filled with Love, is the most precious gift of all.

The nightmare of Maya's stroke never left me.

When it happened again it was worse.

When it happened a third time, I began to wonder if my love for her had made me her enemy as well as her friend.

It is true that each time she recovered.

Each time she seemed just as happy. But each stroke left her a little more feeble.

I felt selfish.

"It is true," said Dr. Mike, "that many people do put a dog to sleep when it starts needing special care."

But I was willing to give up everything for Maya.

"Then it comes down to quality of life."

He assured me that she was in no pain—she was not suffering—that it may not happen again.

He reminded me that all I was willing to do for her was helping to keep Maya alive.

"Please Mike," I said, "if ever you feel I'm being selfish and wrong to Maya—promise you'll tell me."
He promised.

My announcement did not really surprise my friends.

Still, I explained to them that I felt it was wrong to tax Maya's aging body.

She was still capable of staying in for four or five hours at a time, with no discomfort.

But a movie or a downtown dinner did not mean as much to me as Maya's comfort.

If anyone wanted to have dinner with me, we would have to go near my house so I could be back for Maya within two hours.

And no movie was that important.

As for work—

I would break it up into small segments so I could be home in time for Maya.

If not—I would turn it down.

Never mind that my career came to a slow-down—and later to a stop.

Never mind that the friends and family members who said they understood, secretly thought I had "gone off the deep end."

It didn't matter.

My rides with Maya mattered more.

For these car rides, had taken the place of our walks.

Oh, we would still walk a few houses down the block and back.

But I felt that, in her mind, Maya yet remembered the miles and miles of long walks of our past.

And besides, she loved those little hamburgers so very, very much.

How could a hamburger be such a beautiful thing?

Especially these little hamburgers! They were so small and flat that they almost looked painted on their plain, little white buns.

The restaurant they came from seemed to have been there forever.

It was a plain, small, white tile building on the corner of Hunter Boulevard, not far from a lovely little park.

Maya and I used to spend Sunday afternoons in that park. Together, we would watch families play on the swing sets and monkey bars.

One August evening, soon after Maya had turned fifteen, I met my friend Peg in the park. She brought with her some of these little burgers, with some tiny "shoestring fries."

Those burgers were magical. Smothered with onions, pickles, mustard and ketchup, they were truly a feast.

On the way home, I bought a couple of plain ones for Maya.

I think the magic must have been in the old grill,

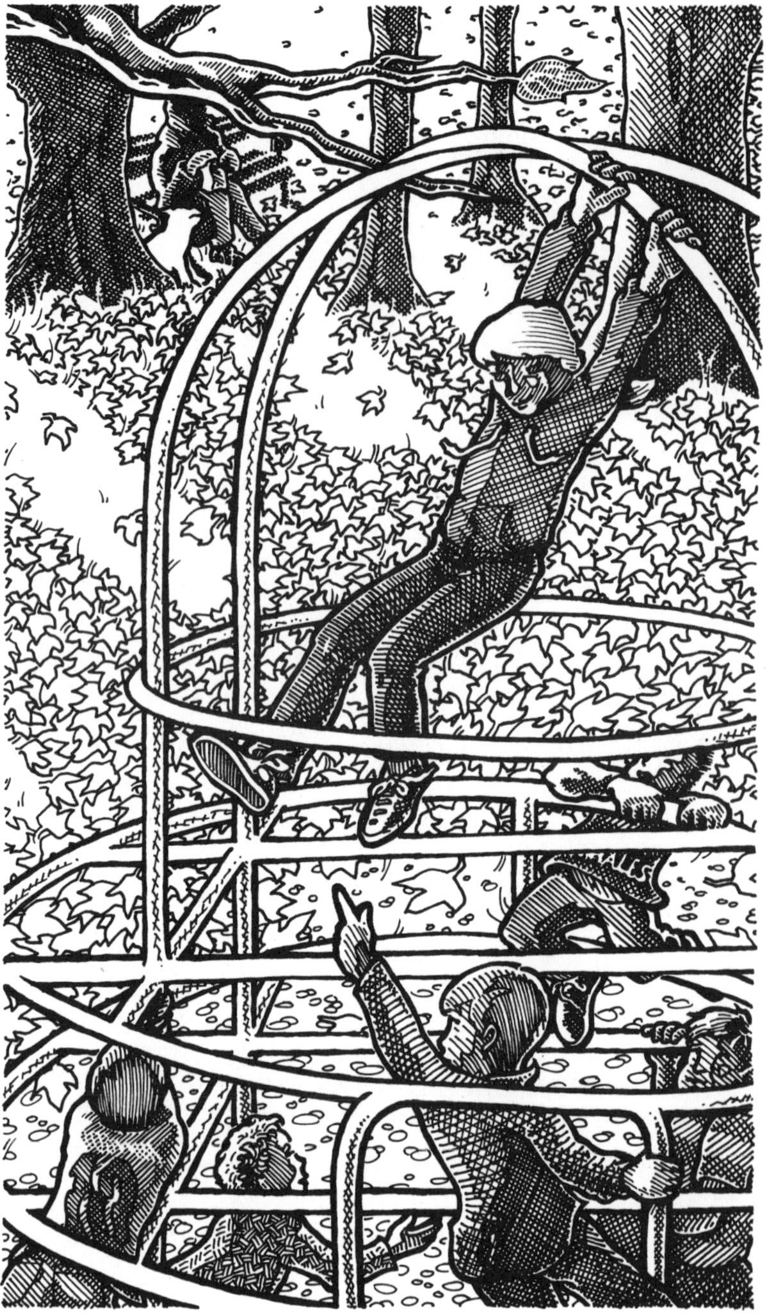

or the way the lady who cooked them, kept flattening 'em down with her spatula, 'til they were almost paper thin.

Whatever the magic, Maya was as delighted as a pirate who had found treasure.

If the burgers were not exactly my idea of treasure, the days that followed were.

For everyday that followed, until the snow came, Maya and I would drive to the corner of Hunter.

Her eyes would never leave the door of the restaurant until I walked out with the small white bag in my hand.

By the time we reached the park, the fries were gone.

I lifted her from the car, and in moments we were on our special bench under the tree—devouring little burgers.

Diamonds and gold could not tempt me to sell the memory of her fifteenth Autumn.

And diamonds and gold could not have bought the magic in those burgers.

For in a year, those forlorn looking little hamburgers, would help to save Maya's life.

Another Spring.

Another Fall.

And with them, the sweetest days of my life.

There was no "us" anymore. We had become one. Our hearts had a single beat. And our lives a single purpose—the care and companionship of each other.

There, in the shade of the giant pines at Cranbrook—one of the loveliest places on earth—Maya waited patiently.

I unfolded the big green Army blanket beneath the young tree, which stood in the shadow of the ancient pines.

A few yards from the car—more than enough of a walk for a sixteen-year-old Dog—and we were both settled on the blanket, together.

The Summer runners and hikers were gone.

Only the sound of the nearby fountain, and the voice of the distant wind, in our ears.

Maya would never look at me, as I was beside her on the blanket.

She kept her eyes straight ahead, as if studying the colors of the changing trees.

And when the geese flew over the pond by the fountain, she would lift her head and listen to their call.

The final currents of summer breeze, hurried away with the smoke from my pipe.

I rested my hand under the collar of Maya's coat, and felt the only true Peace I had ever known in my life.

I had always heard and read about "Oneness" and "Unity." Oneness with nature—Unity with another soul. In my wildest dreams I would never have imagined, that my lesson of Oneness would come through Maya.

Yet, she was all that existed for me.

My family had become so peeved that I "had no interest in anything anymore, except The Dog."

But for me, there *was* nothing but "The Dog."

And when, at her checkups, Dr. Mike would tell me that she was "doing okay," that was my reward and greatest joy.

After a little while, Maya would begin to shift her body, sit up on the blanket, and it would be burger time again.

Folding up the blanket, walking to the car, and lifting her in, we would drive to the burger place.

The girls there knew my order by heart, "Two with everything—four plain—fries."

Then parked by the side of the little park—but not leaving the car as we used to, we would share the close of afternoon.

At home, Maya would sleep, and I would watch her—and pray.

I have always prayed.

And all my life my prayers—like everyone's prayers—have been for mostly selfish things.

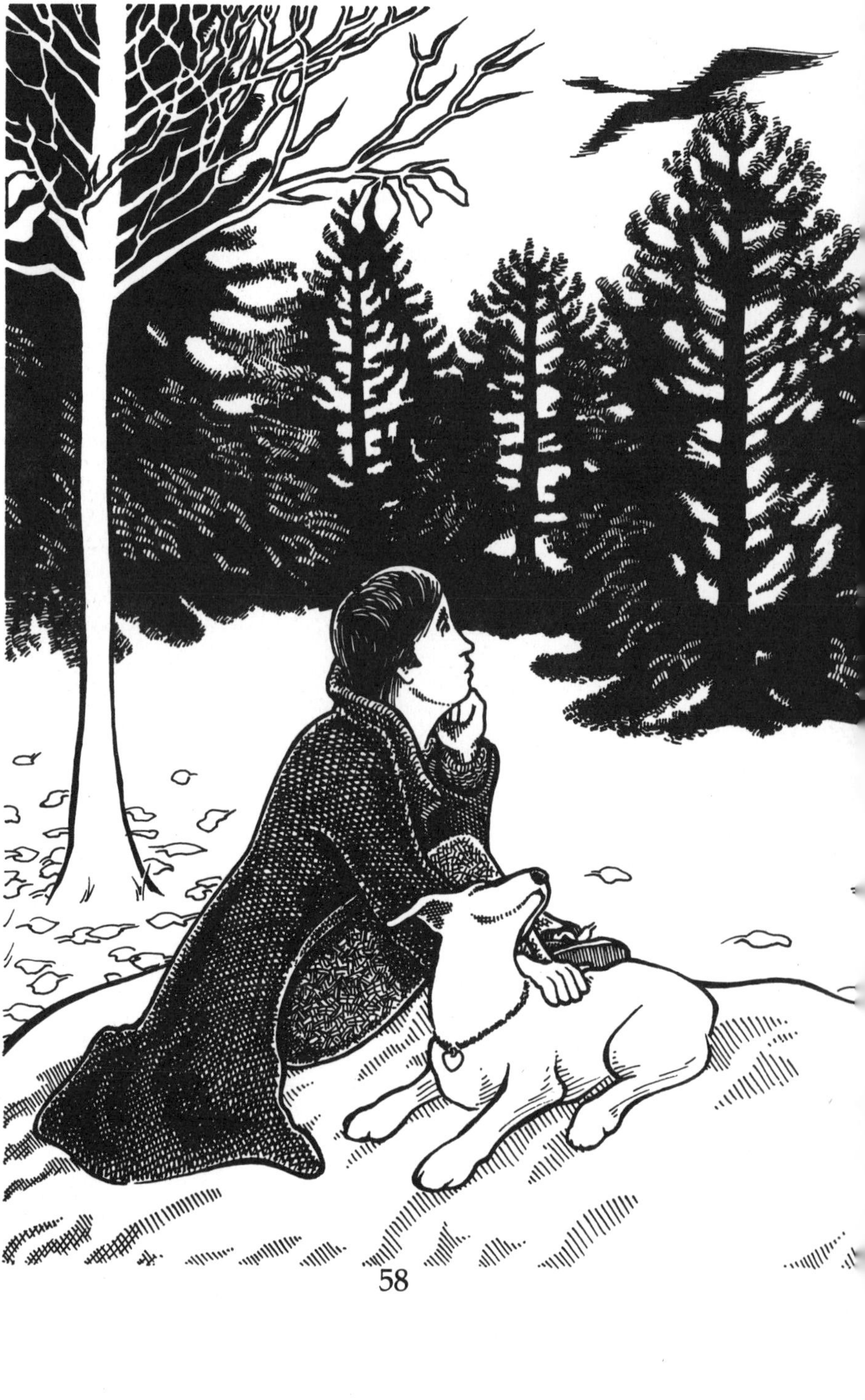

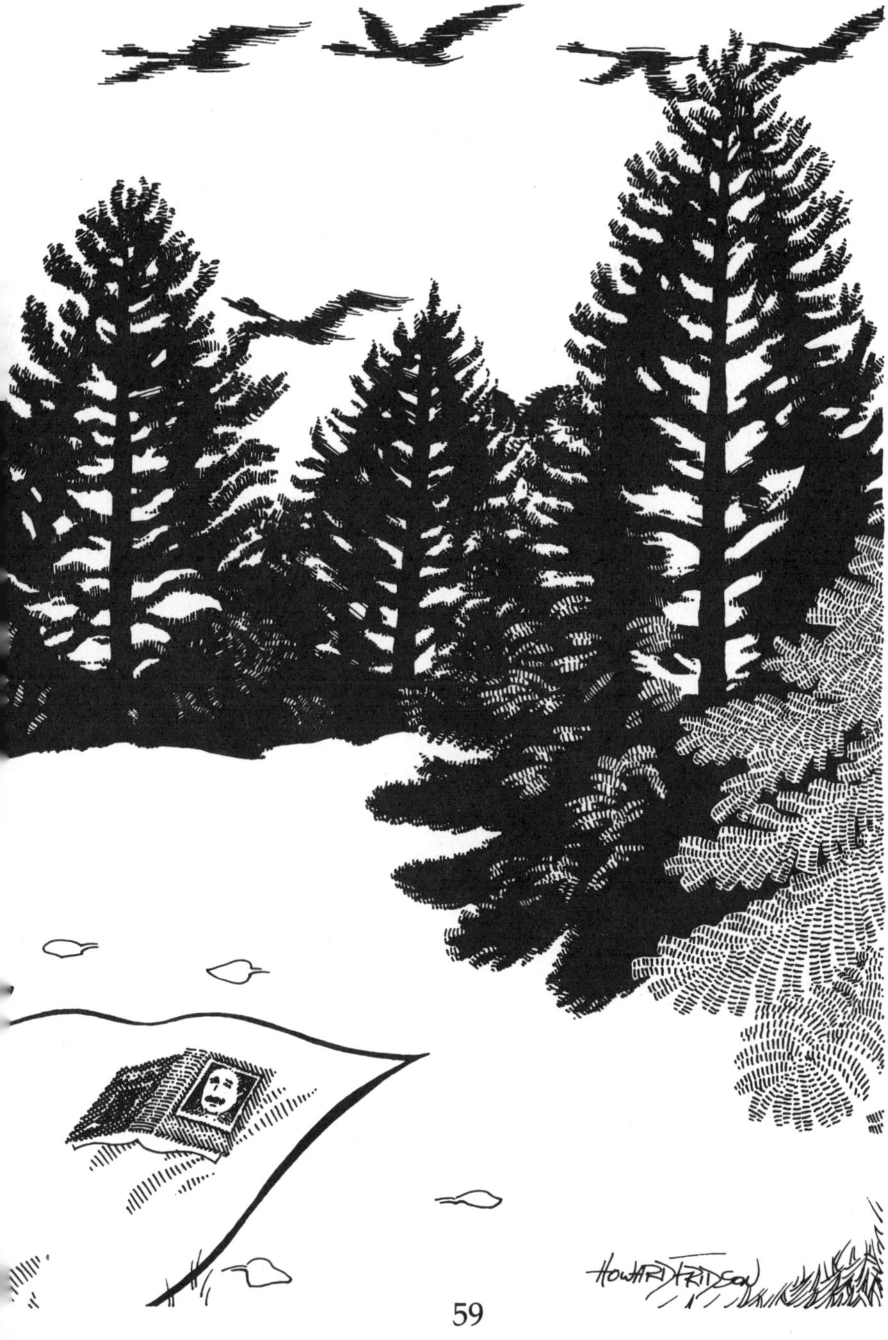
HOWARD FRIDSON

Long prayers for things like success and wealth.
For all I knew, I gave up hope for success and wealth.
My one prayer became just seven words:
"Dear God, Please,
Another Spring,
Another Fall."

"Maya girl, *please* eat something!"

In her entire life, she had never missed a meal. Now she wouldn't even look at food.

I called Dr. Mike.

She was old, and fussy.

If she had lost the taste for boiled burger and no-flavor cereal, perhaps it only made sense.

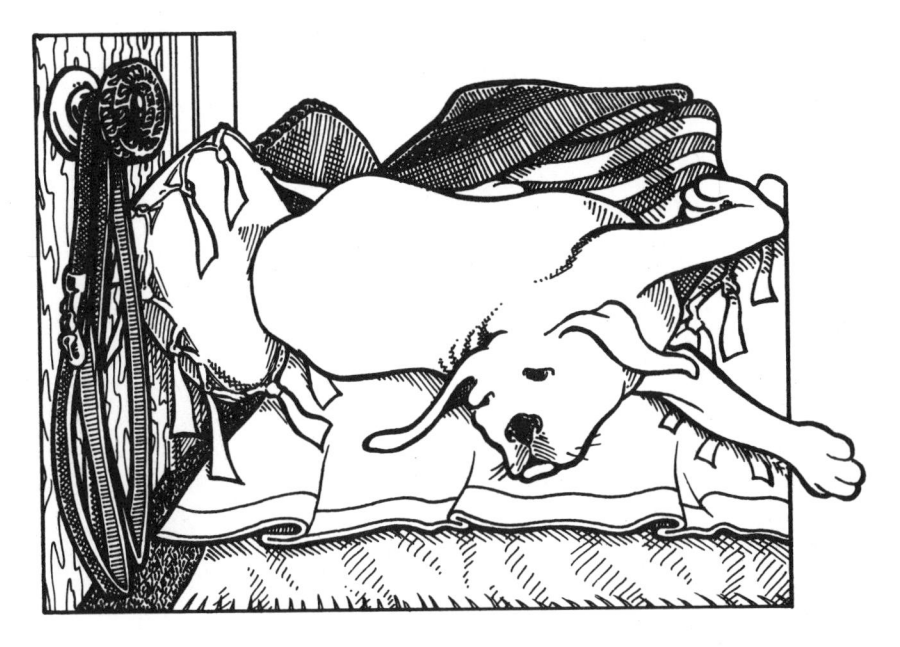

Every day, the little Bar-B-Q near my home had the salt-free chicken ready for me.

Maya ate—but only for a few days.

Something was wrong.

For the first time ever, she did not move when I reached for her leash and her coat.

For the first time ever, she did not want to put them on.

For the very first time, she did not want to go near the car.

We both knew that something was *very* wrong.

She breathed so heavily as we drove to Dr. Mike's.

She only ate a few of the cookies I tried to feed her as we drove.

She wouldn't be still—and there was a terrible frightened look in her eyes.

The second we stepped into the hospital, Maya collapsed on the floor.

For the first time ever,

I had no choice.

I was parted from Maya.

I left Dr. Mike's office, a shell of a person.

I felt as if my heart had been torn out by the roots.

Later that day, Mike gave me the diagnosis.

Every vital level in Maya's body was out of whack—way too high.

There were signs of kidney failure, and the poisons had already entered her system.

I didn't have to say it—Dr. Mike knew that I would do anything, spend any amount to save her.

Whatever was left of me broke into pieces when I saw Maya the next morning.

Just like a person,
she was hooked up to the intravenous.
They were trying to flush her system.
I knew I could not suffer for her,
but I did suffer with her.
I spoke to her,
I held her—
But I could not cheer either of us.
I cannot describe the look in her eyes.
Dr. Mike said there was hope—
But not very much.

And the most crucial moment came
a couple of days later.
The glucose was now not enough to sustain her.
If Maya wanted to live,
She had to eat something.

I had chopped the burger as fine as I could, and cut the chicken into the smallest pieces.

Maya just looked away.

Later, we tried again.

It didn't work.

At home, everything I looked at reminded me of Maya.

The love in the house was gone.

I sat down near the outline of her body, at the spot in the carpet by the piano.

I wept without stopping.

I felt I had discovered what it feels like to die.

The next morning at the hospital I once again begged Maya to eat.

But it was no good at all.

She was in a cage—unable to leave.

On the floor in front of the cage, with the door opened I spoke to her with what felt like my last breath.

"Maya, please, remember our beautiful rides—remember the trees the wind and the fountain. Please get well so we can be together. I promise we'll get burgers every single day."

My words echoed in my ears.

I stopped talking.

A voice inside my mind said, "If I can get her to remember our rides, to know we'll always be together at Cranbrook, she'll eat and she'll live."

I left the hospital in a rush.

The girls at the burger place wondered why my order had changed to "ten-plain."

I didn't answer—just grabbed the bag and went back to Dr. Mike's.

On the floor in front of Maya, I showed her the bag.

I thought I saw a ghost of the gleam in her eyes.

Making a game out of it—I slowly unwrapped one small burger and broke it into little pieces, holding one small wedge between my fingers.

Maya sniffed, and with what little strength she had, delicately took the meat from my hand with her teeth—and swallowed.

Piece by small piece, she ate half the meal.

That night, she ate a full one from the palm of my hand.

Everyday I came morning and night to feed her and comfort her.

But the illness and treatment had taken its toll.

The arthritis had settled into her legs so badly, that she had to be supported to walk. She could hardly stand on her own.

And there were levels in her system which were dangerously high—three times normal.

On every street the Christmas lights brightened the shimmering snow.

From the windows, the neighborhood Christmas trees reminded me of the emptiness at home.

When I was not at the hospital, I was by the phone.

It rang just a few days before Christmas.
The voice was Dr. Mike's.
I listened, hung up, and called Peg.
She could hardly understand what I was saying—I was almost wild with tears and laughter.
"Peg," I said, "Maya's coming home!"

A mile of medicine bottles lined up on the kitchen counter.

There was a pill for everything. Lungs, kidneys, legs, and things that Dr. Mike explained to me, but which I didn't really understand.

Getting Maya to take her thirty pills a day became a challenge and a game.

First peanut butter, then chocolate frosting, then ice cream were used to "disguise" the pills. But she soon caught on. And as soon as she saw me returning from the kitchen, she would grimace and wrinkle up her eyes, and stick her tongue out as if trying to eject a pill. In and out of her mouth the pills would bounce, until they were gone. But I always felt that she knew in her heart, that the medicine was helping to keep us together.

My big fear came at mealtimes. Everyday I made trips to one of the little restaurants that had the things she would eat.

The little burgers were always on the menu. I would drive home as quickly as I could so they would still be hot.

We pretended it was one of our park picnics. I ate with her on the floor in the front room. We were always in the front room now, because she still could not walk very much.

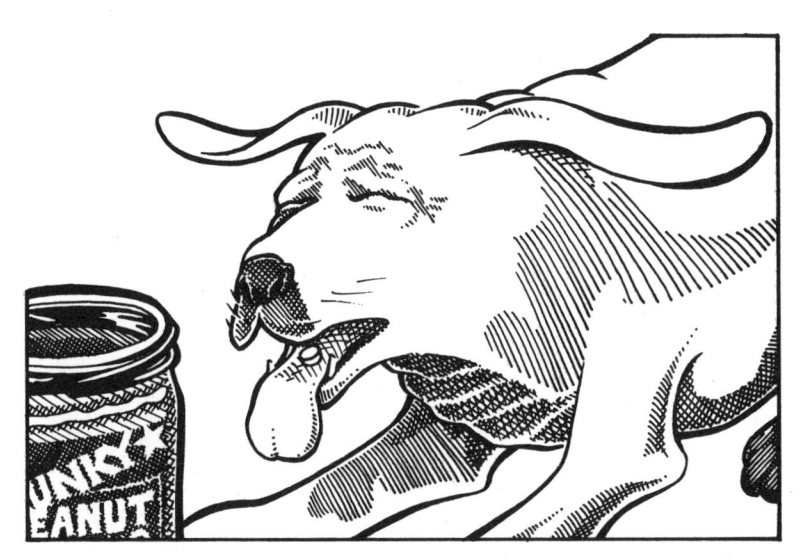

There, near her window on the world, my heart would stand still until I saw her take that first bite.

Even then, I lived in fear that she would grow tired of the burgers. The little Bar-B-Q made me special chicken. And my friend Al, at the Italian restaurant, even reduced the price on the noodles and sauce that Maya grew to love. Everyone knew I was trying to keep her alive.

If they didn't see me for a few days, the first thing they would ask when I came again was, "Is the Dog all right?" Al even suggested other things that we could try to feed her.

Everyone was kind to me.

At night, I lifted Maya in my arms, and placed her at the door of the bedroom.

When she slept I slept—when she woke I awoke. The days began and ended with Maya.

I knew I would never leave her again.

Another Spring.

From the shelter of our home, we watched the beauty of the Earth being reborn.

We were saving every step, cherishing every moment.

The big green blanket spread on the front porch. And now the children were the ones who came up and down the ramp, so they could pet the Big Dog at the yellow house.

With the least activity, and less people in my life than ever, I felt fuller and most fulfilled. The music in my heart, stayed there. It was shared only in a glance, by the priceless creature that had cost me $8—sixteen years ago.

Maya was walking well enough again. I didn't have to carry her around, or outside anymore.

And that beautiful Spring became a Summer of Grace.

We would meet Time together.

Of course, all dogs fear the thunder and lightning of rain storms. And although Maya would have given her life to defend me from danger, she became the world's biggest baby at the sound of a clap of thunder.

Why then, was she breathing so heavily, almost hysterical with fear, even after the storm had stopped?

Why wouldn't she stand still, insisting on pacing the house over and over, even forgetting about the delicate condition of her legs?

Why couldn't I calm her?

Why did this go on for five hours, until dawn?

I called Dr. Mike.

New pills were added to the collection in the kitchen.

These were pills that humans could take.

These were pills for Maya's heart.

Another Fall.

There were no more rides.

The big green blanket lay on the floor of our little screen porch. There in the late afternoons of Autumn, I sat with Maya looking out into the yard.

Her ears still perked up at the sound of the distant geese.

And the wind still nestled the golden red leaves. But these were the leaves of the sheltering vines that covered the screens of the porch.

Water and treats were nearby.

And when she wanted to go in, I placed the large beach towel under her stomach, and gently lifted her hind legs off the ground.

Using her own, yet strong front legs—with me as her back legs—we wheelbarrowed to the place in the hall which had become Maya's real home.

I still recall wondering why she fell at that dip of the land in the backyard. She had never fallen there before, and it was only a slight curve in the ground. But it was not the land, it was her legs, that caused the fall.

Maya had never given up. But her back legs did. They were of no use to her now.

But she was still happy. Still content, and not at all suffering. There was no pain.

So I became her legs.

The lady at the linen store wondered if I was furnishing a new home. I would never have told her that all those blankets and pillows were for a Dog.

On the floor of the hall in the center of the house, the blankets and pillows made a couch for Maya.

She wouldn't get stiff or be sore, because the blankets were soft.

Pillows covered the walls, so she could lay against them.

Whatever position she wanted to shift to, the blankets piled four deep, would cushion her.

I could see her from the bedroom, from the shower, from the dining room, from the kitchen. If I were in the front room, or at the piano, I would still only be four steps away.

We were near the porch and the ramp to the yard.

And through the front door, she could still see the world she had known all of her life.

She could still bark at the mailman, with her huge brave growl.

She could still see the sun.

She could still hear the music from the records which kept us constant company.

And when I read or talked on the phone, or just wanted to be with Maya, there was room for me beside her on that couch.

In the last picture of Maya that I ever took, she is laying on her couch.

She is an Old Dog, in an old body.

She hasn't walked for months.

But on her face, is the smile of a newborn baby.

For she really had become a baby again.

In those months, whatever a baby would have needed, Maya needed too.

Some days were wonderful.

Others were very hard.

But once, at the end of one of the hard days, something happened.

We had come in from a difficult trip to the yard.

Panting and exhausted, we both collapsed breathless on the blankets.

I felt awful, wondering if I was wrong to fight the inevitable.

But later, in the silver of evening on the porch, Maya looked at me with the look of an Angel.

I knew I could read the thought in her mind.

With the calm Autumn all around us, her thought was, "Don't ever feel badly. This has all been worth it. We love each other, and time can never change that."

"How can you stay in the house so long?"

"Don't you feel cooped up—like a prisoner?"

"Aren't you going crazy, there all by yourself?"

People asked me these questions over and over.

The fact is that I made some promises.

I promised myself that for as long as Maya lived, I would never leave her again.

And I promised God, that if Maya could die peacefully, in her sleep, with no pain, that I would never again burden Him by asking for anything.

Very few friends understood.

My best friend Tom understood, and came to visit when he could.

And Dr. Mike understood, and did an extraordinary thing. One day he said that since I could no longer lift her, and since she was now so petrified of the car, he would come to my home to check on Maya every week or so.

It was a long drive for him, but he would come with pills and his stethescope, and whatever other equipment he needed to care for Maya.

He took my calls at the office—sometimes four or five calls a day, on the rough days.

The amount of money he accepted was only for

the medicine. For a whole year, he would not take anything for his services.

Mike was there for Maya and for me, at a time when both of us needed him more than anything else in our lives.

My work had stopped almost entirely. If I needed to send a letter, I wrote it out for Susie, my secretary. After I would mail it to her, she would type it, sign it, and mail it for me.

On days when I had about an hour's worth of errands to do, I would do them one at a time, in fifteen or twenty minute shifts. After each one, I would come back home to check on Maya.

And, of course, I never left the house while she was still sleeping from the night before. She had begun sleeping longer and longer now.

There were days when she might sleep until four or five in the afternoon. Mostly these were times when she was up 'til early morning. Either she had been restless, or needing to go outside many times in a row—sometimes eight or ten—because of her medications.

Still, it was no chore or problem.

When she was awake, I was never more than a few feet away.

While she slept, I watched her—often sitting close beside her, at *her* side, as she had for me all the days of her life.

On her restless nights, which became her long sleeping days, I barely slept at all. Indeed, there were no days and nights anymore, just our life together, which was being given to us a moment at a time.

Moments more precious to me now, than anything I may have been missing in the outside life of the world.

My world was a complete one, with nothing missing at all.

I had once asked a woman to join me for dinner. I said we would bring in some food from a fine restaurant, put on some good music, and enjoy each other's company.

Of course she wanted to know why I would prefer this to dining out.

I told her about Maya.

She couldn't believe her ears.

Then I asked her, "What if your mother was very old and very ill, and could not get along without you. Would you leave the house just to have dinner?"

"But that's a person! Not an animal!" was her answer.

On that day, I stopped trying to explain to anyone about my devotion to Maya.

I went about things in my own way.

I don't really blame that woman or people like her, for their lack of compassion. After all, if my own family and friends could not understand, why should strangers even try.

Although certain friends faded away during Maya's last days, I did learn who my truest friends were. And I made a new true friend in Dr. Mike.

What I will not understand as long as I live, is why some people value the life of a person over the life of an animal. After all, is not life sacred in every form?

How many times have we heard people say that "Even when a swallow falls, God knows."

Often now I think, "If God with all His problems, still knows when a swallow falls, then is not the life of that swallow as precious as my own?"

And I wonder too, "Why couldn't more people understand, that the life of a Dog who lived only for me, was as sacred to me as the swallow is to God."

Thanksgiving dinner was a disaster.

The only reason I went at all is that my Dear Old Uncle, who had been ill on and off for a year, wanted to treat the family to a nice dinner at a fancy restaurant.

So I went, and as a gesture of thanks, I invited Dr. Mike to join me.

Although I tried to be cheerful, I was a knot inside. I didn't like leaving Maya.

To make things worse, an argument broke out during dinner. My Uncle was obviously unwell, but he took it out on me.

I endured, but was so embarrassed.

It was impossible to eat.

At the end of dinner I stormed away with the comment that "I left a sick Dog only to be made more miserable."

I rushed home with a doggie bag filled with turkey and stuffing.

I held Maya as she ate, and was glad that at least this much joy came out of a horrible experience.

Dr. Mike had followed me home to check on Maya. Her heartbeat was still irregular—but seemed to be stabilizing more.

I apologized to him for the lousy evening—but he understood.

We had coffee, and he left.

I felt as if I was in agony. My nerves were gone. My back was in pain from Maya's weight. And I had developed a hernia from the many times of lifting, and my system of being Maya's legs.

I couldn't have cared less if I ever talked to my family again.

Or my friends.

Because no one had ever really shown me that they *truly* understood.

But I looked at Maya, and she seemed happy and content.

Her eyes were soft, and focused upon me.

I held her—

and hugged her,

and looked back

into her eyes.

With her head in my hands, I said in words that would hardly come, "Come on Old Girl, let's make it to Christmas."

In the beginnings and endings of Life, animals and people become equal. Neither know when, and neither know how.

It was the last week in November, and Dr. Mike seemed very satisfied. Maya's heartbeat sounded better—more stable and even.

Yet, over dinner, he gently asked me what I wanted when Maya passed away.

He listed the choices: farm burial, pet cemetery, cremation. We discussed them all, but I knew for a long time that Maya would be cremated. The same as I desire for myself when my time comes.

The mixture of joy and sorrow, which we find in having loved truly, stayed in my mind that night.

For some reason, I thought back to Halloween, which had always been my favorite time—even since childhood.

Maya and I always made a special occasion of Halloween. She ran from the window to the door as the children came up the walk. She sniffed at the huge bowls of candy which we handed out by the fistful. Then, she ran back from the door to the window waiting for the chance to bark again at the endless streams of small children, whom she loved so much.

Last year, on Halloween—to save her legs—I sat her by the open door where she could watch me and the children on the porch, without having to run back and forth.

This never kept her from barking endlessly, until the last ghost had come and gone.

This year she could see it all from her "couch."

The door was open,

The children came,

Some even came inside to pet her.

But Maya just fell asleep—

Halloween was not special this year.

And now, on the brink of December, the look on Dr. Mike's face had changed to concern.

He could hear fluid in Maya's lungs—lungs which may have become to old to cope.

In fact, it seemed that all of Maya's age, had defeated Time in that one moment.

Mike and I went immediately to buy a vaporizer, which stayed on day and night.

Snow was on the ground. And I was continuously clearing the ramp and the yard as in years past.

But I wanted to spare Maya even the few steps down the ramp.

I began to make plans to turn our little back porch into a giant litter box. This would certainly make the Winter easier on her.

The new red sweater was my symbol of our braving the Winter ahead.

I was always careful to see that Maya's smile showed that there was no pain for her.

Her dinners and snacks were all devoured with the zeal of a pup.

And it was not unusual, that morning twenty days before Christmas, to awake at noon and find her still asleep.

It was when the heavy breathing started, later, that I thought something might be wrong.

Dr. Mike gave permission to give her an extra pill, and call again later if I needed to.

By the time I realized that Maya had not changed position—or asked for breakfast, Dr. Mike had left the office to do his Holiday shopping.

Maya's breathing became heavier, and her eyes looked at me with love and hope—but also with stillness.

She swallowed some ice cream, and the drops of water I placed on her tongue.

But finally in desperation—I placed an emergency call to the unlisted number of Dr. Mike's partner—who told me he thought it was time.

He would come immediately, and the decision would be mine.

A short time passed, and dusk had become evening when the phone rang.

It was Mike.

"Mike," I said, "She's dying."

His voice sounded as if he couldn't believe it.

I cradled Maya's head in my lap—and sang to her in a whisper, the soft silly and tender songs of our years of joy.

My mind told me that the thing I feared the most would now have to be.

As my lips told her endlessly that I loved her, my heart prayed one last time for freedom from having to do this thing.

It was night—

And Mike was at the door with tears in his eyes.

As I let him in

I told him.

It had been only moments before, when Maya, with dignity, and peacefulness, and that wonderful smile on her face, quietly left forever.

There was no light outside.
There was no moon.
There were no stars.

Maya was in her place, in the back seat of the car. But this time, it was Mike who had carried her from the house.

She was wrapped in the old pea coat which I had worn with her all our years together.

On all our walks,

on all our rides,

during all her healthy young years,

and during all the hard times of her old years.

First I would put Maya's old plaid coat on her, then put the old pea coat on myself.

Peg and my sister made me stop wearing that old coat a few years ago.

True, it looked pretty bad. It had been mended and patched many times. In most spots, the material was almost gone. So Peg and my sister teamed up to make me promise not to wear the coat in public anymore. And I never did—when I was with either of them.

But when Maya and I went to Cranbrook or the park, to the cider mill for donuts, or for burgers—and

when we walked among the Autumn trees, I always wore my pea coat.
    Now she lay, resting and wrapped in my coat, for our last ride together.
    We were driving to Dr. Mike's office.
    He followed us in his car.
    She was not afraid this time—
    But I still spoke to her quietly,
    Because I felt that she could still hear me.
    Once inside Dr. Mike's I thanked him, shook his hand, and left quickly.
    She looked so different to me in that final moment.
    How afraid of death we all are—only because we don't really understand what it is.
    Yet, sometimes I feel I do understand a little.
    For if I did not exactly die that night, I know I was certainly not alive as I drove home from Dr. Mike's, walked into my house, looked at Maya's blankets,
    And closed the door behind me.

No wise man who ever lived, could truly comfort the heart that has lost what it held most dear.

Most people have experienced the loss of a loved one. So they try, each in their own way, to make you feel they understand how sad you are.

The world understands less, the pain of losing an animal.

This is because many people have never felt for themselves, the true love of an animal. So, you can not really expect these people to realize that your love for a pet may be greater than your love for the dearest people in your life.

The bond is different, and can never be put into words.

It is a bond that only The Heart understands.

When my mother died, I continued with all my will power, to work and compose. There was a lot in my life that had to be done, so I tried to carry on.

When Maya left, I found no will power left. There was no work, or music to compose. Maya had become my life. There was little to carry on for.

The people who had been concerned—the restaurant owners and the grocer—all said they were sorry. It was nice of them. But it actually made things worse, because they would then ask, "Are you getting another dog?"

No one had ever asked me, "Are you getting another mother?"

This is what I mean about the understanding of the world when a pet passes on.

Love—in any form—can never be replaced.

Perhaps the saddest sound in the world is the cry of the geese as they fly South for the winter. They sound even sadder to me, now that Maya is gone. Yet as I watch them soar in their elegant and graceful V against the clouds, I try to remember that Maya's soul can also soar—free as the geese and the clouds.

As I have been remembering, the New Year has quietly come.

I still do not know how long it will take me to get used to living without Maya.

But I do know for sure, that no rich man's fortune could ever buy even one of my memories of Maya. They are just that precious to me.

Of course there is a Rose watching tenderly over her place.

And I don't think it is so very strange at all, that even though I can no longer hold her, or hear her ears flap, or sing to her, or look into the most loving brown eyes in the world, or help her get comfortable, or feed her chocolates, or touch her paw, or see her smile, or listen to the slow quiet song of her breath— or watch her sleep. . .

That even though I really know she is gone. . .

Still,

I feel Maya peacefully, and happily, at my side.

For as you know,

Maya is *always* at my side.

The Rose seemed to take forever to open.

Perhaps it is because each day now seemed to take forever to pass.

White ice replaced the amber leaves, forcefully clinging to the screens of the porch.

It felt as if the ice had enclosed my heart as well.

The ramps were covered over with layers of smooth snow. But I thought I could see the imprint of Maya's footsteps.

It must have just been the reflection of our tree's bare branches, as the moon shone through them onto the ramp below.

The night, the house, the yard, were as still as if time had ended.

But The Rose lived longer than any I had ever seen.

I had placed it in a small, old vase, that used to belong to my mother.

On the floor, near Maya's blankets, it became a symbol of my love for them both.

I know most people think of my feelings, and actions, for Maya as being extreme. Maybe even "extreme" is an understatement.

But I have always been extreme in everything, and now, depression had caved in on me.

My Dear Old Uncle had always thought that I was a little crazy. But, he had always a kind word and made an effort to understand.

He was beginning to worry. "Just do something," he said. "Anything—but try to break out of it. It may take you a year to begin to feel all right—but try."

Two months went by, and I received an offer to perform again.

A million-dollar restaurant, a grand piano, a tuxedo, being with people again.

I played, but did not really hear the music.

And each Saturday night, even now, people see The Rose that lies on the piano.

The women often say how lovely it is—deep red against the shiny black.

The crowds come and go.

The music lingers for only a moment.

But I see a Rose that lasts forever.

And a face that was my world.

And each Rose becomes the one that opened petal by petal—
Taking seventeen years to
Bloom and Blossom

I saw Maya today,
Young and alive and
smiling the smile
of Freedom.

It is almost June,
and six months
have crawled by
so slowly that
I feel I have lived
a century with no heart.

My ears and eyes
Tell me it is Spring—
almost Summer—

But my spirit feels
The chill of wet Winter,
and the day I placed Maya's ashes
beneath the tree
at Cranbrook.

No matter where I travel
in the world,
I can always come home to find
The peace I knew
when Maya lay beside me
on the big Army blanket.

So many days since December,
I have come to the tree
with a Rose.
So many times
I placed a Rose in the snow—
and watched the petals
move in the force of the Winter wind.

And on the first of these many visits,
the carillon in the nearby church
sent the voices of her chimes
to console me
in the white frost.

As the seasons changed,
Bird songs replaced
The ringing of the chimes.

And on sunny afternoons,
I thought I could see
Maya, lying calm and happy—
Her head lifted to the sun—
The breeze
brushing her eyelashes
and ruffling her greying hair.

Yet today—
On the birth of Summer—
as I approach the tree—

She was standing
not sitting.

She was young,
not old.

She was well,
not ill.

She was able to
walk and jump and run,
for she was
no longer crippled.

And she was waiting
For me
Beneath the tree
to remind me of my love—
and help me through
my loneliness.

And so, today,
I stayed and sat
once more beneath
our tree.

And once more I leave a single Rose
for Maya.

For I know
that I may come to our tree
many more times
for the rest of my days.

But I know that Maya
Was telling me today,
That her spirit lays,
Happily,
Beneath a tree in
The Garden of God.

She is there in the Sun
with the Spirits of all the Dogs
we have loved, and lost
so soon.

There,
in the Brightness
of God's own Light—
They think of us,

As God

Shows them to the Angels,
Singing of Loyalty
and Pure
Eternal Love.

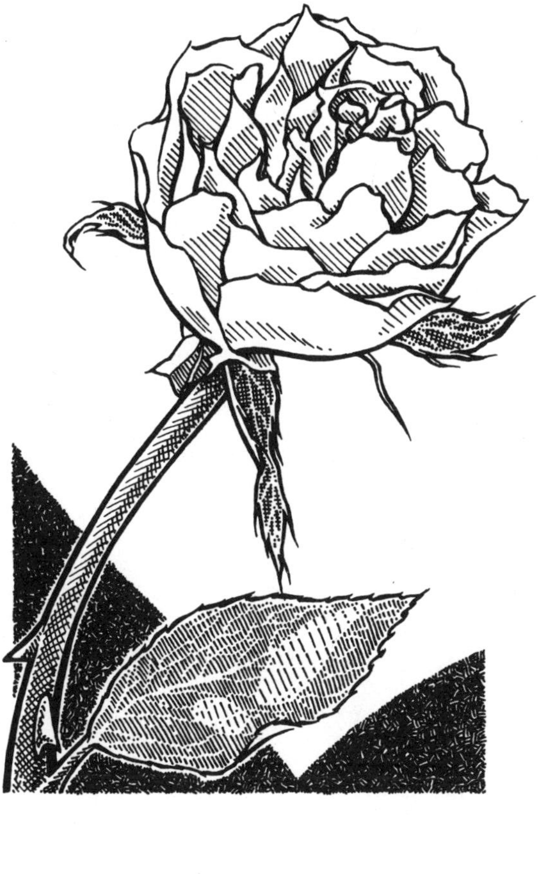

My Dear Maya

AN AFTERWORD

In a moment of greatest joy, there is often a seed of sorrow. In a moment of happy gain, there is sometimes the seed of loss.

When we go to choose a pet, we feel we are choosing a life's companion. When we choose that one special pair of eyes, from all those that watch us longingly, our hearts know that here is someone that may grow dearer to us than even our best of friends.

But somewhere deep inside, I believe we feel something telling us, that forever will not be possible for our new friend, except in memory.

Perhaps, it is really this way with everyone we love. But this thought does not make it easier to accept the short life span of our animal companions.

So many books have been written about the pain of losing a loved one. Yet, of all the books I have read, only a few mention the loss of a pet. Even then, there is only a sentence or two at most.

The world is only beginning to realize how important pets are to young and old alike. And the Human-Animal Emotional Bond is just beginning to be explored by psychologists. It is natural then, to feel that no one can really understand your loss and your grief.

If your experience is similar to mine, you may find yourself constantly occupied with thoughts of your late pet. Even now, I often dream of Maya. These are living, realistic dreams which feel as if she is actually visiting me.

I feel it is crucial not to suppress the thoughts, the feelings, or the dreams. You must talk to someone. Do not hide your feelings because most people will think, "it was only a pet."

Happily, there are groups and hotlines springing up all over the country, which are devoted to helping people through the devastating loss of a pet. One such group is The Pet Loss Support Hotline, at the University of California, Davis. Their counselors can be reached from 6:30p.m. to 9:30p.m. Pacific Time, Monday through Friday. The phone number is (916) 752–4200. You may write them at the following address:

>	The Human-Animal Program
>	School of Veterinary Medicine
>	University of California
>	Davis, California 95616

This group, and others like it, are there to help you both before and after your pet passes away. Please realize that if you express your feelings at the beginning of your pet's illness or ageing process, then you may be more emotionally equipped to handle the absence of your dear companion.

An extensive list of hotlines, support groups, and counselors, located throughout the United States and Canada, is published by:

The Delta Society
Century Building
Third Floor
321 Burnett Avenue South
Renton, Washington 98055-2569
Phone: (206) 226-7357

For a small donation, The Delta Society will also send you lists of literature, video and audio tapes, concerning many aspects of the Human-Animal Bond.

For those whose dogs and cats will eventually suffer from arthritis, or paralysis, I urge you to contact:

K-9 Cart Company
532 Newton Road
Berwyn, Pennsylvania 19312
Phone: (215) 644-6624

This unique company manufactures special carts, that can support an animal's legs with wheels. These are made to order, and can add mobility, and years, to a pet's life.

It may not be the best of formal etiquette for an author to directly address his reader, but in a sense I feel very close and connected to everyone who has held this book in their hands, and who has shared my story of Maya with me.

I can only hope that this sharing has helped you in some way. And I hope that you will not mind just a few more words of advice.

Just as you alone can decide the issue of your pet's final day, and the issue of your pet's final resting place, there will be other issues upon your pet's passing, that only you can decide.

When do you remove your pet's belongings from their usual place in the house?

It took me a year to fold Maya's blankets and pack up her pillows. Now, her toys remain in their spot by the fireplace, and her leash still hangs on the knob of the hall closet door.

What about getting another pet?

Some veterinarians and counsellors recommend choosing a new pet almost immediately. Some say to wait for the grieving process to take its course.

In my own case, I have not yet even considered it.

These are truly personal decisions, and I believe are not to be forced.

I also believe that every dog should have a coat. Maya had three. There was her original plaid coat for Fall, and a heavy lined one for Winter. She also had a raincoat which made her look like Sherlock Holmes.

Dogs may love the elements, but cold weather and snow and frost are not always their friends.

Above all, please do not let your dog roam free.

You may think that dogs are happy with their freedom, running free. But if something should happen, you will not be able to forgive yourself.

Your dog will be just as happy being loved by being close.

All animals are a treasure. We must treat them as we would rare jewels.

MARTIN SCOT KOSINS began his composing career in 1971 with the encouragement of famed cellist Gregor Piatigorsky. Since then, his music has been performed and recorded internationally by artists such as Sir Neville Marriner, Laurindo Almeida, Bud Shank and The Detroit Symphony Orchestra. He has composed for numerous chamber music groups and ballet, and is a recipient of the ASCAP Composers Award.

As record producer, Martin has headed projects by John Carradine, Loretta Swit, Keith Carradine, The Ink Spots, Al Hibbler, and Count Basie Alumni, and has also produced for CBS records.

His commercial credits include music for companies such as BMW and Gund.

As a writer, Martin Scot Kosins has authored many articles for newspapers and periodicals. MAYA'S FIRST ROSE is his first published book.

Since Maya's passing, Martin is reemerging as one of the foremost café pianists and entertainers.

HOWARD FRIDSON'S animals peer with human expression from canvasses and walls around the country. Since graduating from Wayne State University's Fine Arts Program, he has hung from scaffolding painting two-story tall sea gulls, and squinted through a magnifying glass effecting miniature portraits for a Victorian doll house.

In more conventional scale are countless murals in and outside of the Michigan area, as well as illustrations for Special Education material and other books.

Howard also spends a portion of his time in the Berkley, Michigan School District where he lectures, draws, and drives car pool along with his wife Cathy for their three sons Nathan, Blake and Russell.

The Fridsons live in Huntington Woods, Michigan with their dog Two-ey, who at the command "paint," will take a brush from a can and dab at a makeshift easel.

BURL IVES is the world's most beloved Balladeer. He is also one of the most respected actors of our time, having won the Academy Award for his role in "The Big Country."

His recordings of American Folk Music have sold in the millions, and are as legendary as the man himself.

Mr. Ives has lent his talent and support to many worthy causes, and approaches these efforts with the same sincerity found in his memorable performances.